SOUTHAMPTON
TO
BOURNEMOUTH

Vic Mitchell and Keith Smith

Design – Deborah Goodridge

First published May 1987

ISBN 0 906520 42 8

© *Middleton Press, 1987*

Typeset by CitySet - Bosham 573270

Published by Middleton Press
        Easebourne Lane
        Midhurst, West Sussex
        GU29 9AZ
    ☎ *073 081 3169*

Printed & bound by Biddles Ltd,
        Guildford and Kings Lynn

CONTENTS

GEOGRAPHICAL SETTING

Southampton has two important features which have always helped to keep it amongst Britain's leading ports. Firstly, it stands on high flood-free ground at the confluence of the deep waters of the Rivers Itchen and Test. Secondly, it has the almost unique advantage of four high tides per day, due to the Isle of Wight splitting the rising sea as it moves eastwards along the English Channel.

After crossing the River Test, the railway route rises onto the undulating plateau of the New Forest. Now largely an infertile area, much of the forest was destroyed by medieval shipbuilders.

The small Lymington River is crossed just before reaching Brockenhurst, the Lymington branch crossing it again near its mouth. The crossing of four small rivers precedes the bridges over the River Avon and River Stour, either side of Christchurch. The line then climbs onto the high sandy ground on which Bournemouth and its suburbs have grown.

ACKNOWLEDGEMENTS

We are grateful for the help received from the photographers mentioned in the captions and also for the assistance received from Mrs. E. Fisk, G. Croughton, E. Gamblin, Dr. T.A. Gough, R. Randell, N. Stanyon. C.E.G. Townsend and our ever helpful wives

The Ordnance Survey maps reproduced
in this album are to the scale of 25" to 1 mile,
unless otherwise stated.

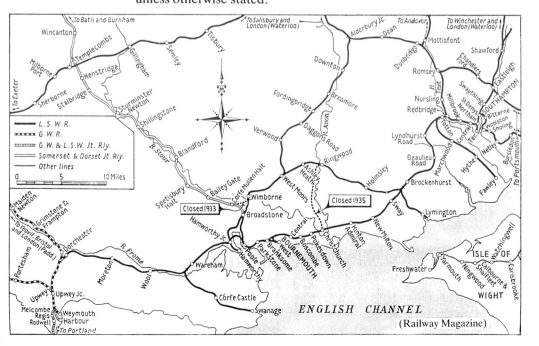
(Railway Magazine)

HISTORICAL BACKGROUND

A single line railway between South-ampton and Dorchester via Brockenhurst and Ringwood was opened on 1st June 1847. The terminus at Southampton was close to the present station and was known succes-sively as Blechynden, West and Central. The extension of the line to Southampton Ter-minus was delayed until 29th July, owing to difficulty with the construction of the tunnel. Thus, as at Brighton at this time, all trains from London proceeding further west had to reverse. It was not until July 1858, that a curve at Northam was laid to permit direct running.

The circuitous route to Dorchester was called "Castleman's Corckscrew", Castle-man being a Wimborne solicitor who proposed a route that would link as many towns as possible. Bournemouth was of no consequ-ence at that time but it soon grew and passen-gers had to travel there by way of a branch from Broadstone to Poole, now a goods only line to Hamworthy.

A single line branch from Brockenhurst to Lymington came into use on 12th July 1858 and it was eventually extended to the Pier on 1st May 1884. Doubling of the main line took place in 1857-63.

A branch from Ringwood down to Christ-church was brought into traffic on 13th November 1862 and was extended to Bourne-mouth on 14th March 1870, the terminus eventually being known as Bournemouth East. Bournemouth West opened in 1874 and the connecting line between them fol-lowed in 1888.

The last link in the network, between Brockenhurst and Christchurch, came into use on 5th March 1888. It was built as double track, the section from Christchurch to Bournemouth having been doubled two years earlier.

Although first proposed by the LSWR in 1902, the branch to Fawley from Totton did not come into use until 20th July 1925. It lost its passenger service on 14th February 1966 but remains open for oil and military traffic. All services between Ringwood and Christ-church were withdrawn on 30th September 1935 and passenger trains between Ringwood and Brockenhurst were suspended from 4th May 1964.

A notable event in the history of the route was the introduction of electric traction on 10th July 1967. The electrification included the branch to Lymington Pier but not the Fawley line.

* * * * *

The population of Bournemouth increased dramatically in the final decades of the 19th century, largely as a result of the improve-ments in rail services.

1861	1940
1871	5900
1881	16800
1891	37600

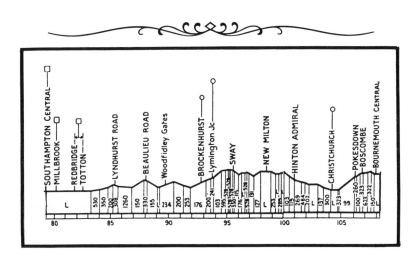

PASSENGER SERVICES

The initial service between Southampton and Dorchester comprised five trains each way. By 1869, there were six journeys on weekdays and three on Sundays, with connections at Ringwood Junction for Christchurch, on weekdays only.

The 1890 service direct to Bournemouth was one of eleven trains each way on weekdays and three on Sundays. By 1910, this had been increased to 17 and 6, respectively. In addition, there were three "Motor Train" journeys from Bournemouth to New Milton and seven to Christchurch. At the other end of the route, there were six extra trains between Southampton and Brockenhurst, some of which were extended to Ringwood.

Pullman cars appeared in some trains between 1890 and 1910 but it was not until July 1931 that the all Pullman "Bournemouth Belle" was introduced.

On 1st July 1910, a through train to Birkenhead via Basingstoke and the GWR commenced operation. It also had through coaches to Manchester, which were detached at Wellington.

Other through services using the route have included direct trains to Kings Cross, Brighton and Bradford, the latter via the Great Central line.

The 1924 weekday timetable showed six trains to Bournemouth from Ringwood via Hurn, fifteen from Waterloo, one from Newcastle, one from Reading, one from Dover via Guildford, one from Birkenhead and some additional local journeys from Brockenhurst.

By the summer of 1938 the service had increased to sixteen fast trains from Waterloo and fourteen slow ones originating from Southampton or beyond with four from Brockenhurst. There were many extras on Fridays and Saturdays to cope with the holiday crowds.

Frequency was reduced during World War II and immediately thereafter but the 1950s brought new peaks in holiday traffic.

The full electric timetable has been operational since 1968. It provides for a basic service of three trains per hour – a fast train from Waterloo calling only at Southampton, where it connects with an all-stations service, and a semi-fast train calling at Christchurch and Brockenhurst, where it connects with the Lymington branch shuttle. Additional journeys are made in the business hours and on summer Saturdays, the latter still including some through workings to Lymington Pier.

Destinations of inter-regional diesel-hauled services have included Newcastle, Manchester, Liverpool and, more recently, Glasgow. The latter also has through coaches to Edinburgh and is named *The Wessex Scot*.

The Poole and Weymouth services will be similarly outlined in a future album.

Lymington Branch

Initially connections were provided with most main line services and by 1890 there were eight journeys on the branch – weekdays only. The 1910 timetable showed ten return trips, although three terminated at the Town station. The Sunday service of three trains was eventually increased to six, although the weekday service was little changed for about 40 years. Sunday trains were withdrawn during World War II but reached a peak of nine return journeys in the mid-1950s, when up to 17 trips were made on weekdays.

A decline in frequency in the early 1960s was compensated for with the introduction of an hourly service in readiness for electrification.

Fawley Branch

The passenger services are best summarised as sparse. In the early years, there were three down and four up workings, weekdays only. They were timed to enable local residents to travel to work in Southampton but when the service was eventually reduced to two return journeys, they at times to suit those working at Fawley.

During the construction of the Anglo American Oil Refinery in 1950, an eleven coach train left Eastleigh at 6.38 each morning with workers. This was at times insufficient and a relief train was added at 6.50 from Southampton.

SOUTHAMPTON

1. Southampton West, known as Blechynden until July 1858, is seen after it had ceased to serve passengers. It became a goods depot – the platform was later dug away and the siding on the left was extended under the awning. On the right is the Corporation Electricity Works, served by a siding which crossed the road, until 1964.
(D. Cullum collection)

2. The second station at Southampton West was brought into use on 1st November 1892 and is seen here with its fully glazed footbridge and famous clock tower.
(Lens of Sutton)

The 1870 edition shows the water-front houses of Western Shore on the right. The station was called Southampton West End for some time.

3. Looking west from the down starting signal in 1931, the proximity of the Test estuary to the line is evident. The SR embarked on a massive 400 acre reclamation project in the early 1930s, which included the deposition of thousands of tons of chalk, from Micheldever and elsewhere, for hardstanding. 146 concrete monoliths weighing about 5000 tons each were sunk at the new waterfront and dredgings were pumped in behind to displace the water. The cranes are seen working to form the new quay side. (Late E. Wallis)

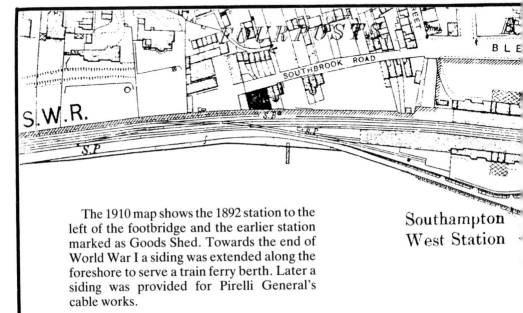

The 1910 map shows the 1892 station to the left of the footbridge and the earlier station marked as Goods Shed. Towards the end of World War I a siding was extended along the foreshore to serve a train ferry berth. Later a siding was provided for Pirelli General's cable works.

Southampton West Station

4. A photograph from March 1934 shows the footbridge being doubled in length to enable four platform lines to be provided. The level crossing in the foreground was abolished and the remaining part of the first station, on the left, was demolished. In the distance the tunnel mouth and the long-lost Congregational Church. (British Rail)

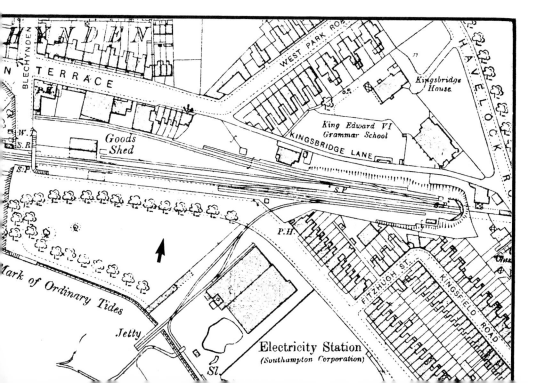

5. The third station was completed in 1935 and was officially Southampton Central from 7th July. The suffix was dropped in 1967, the year after the Terminus station had closed. The bus bears the legend "South Western Hotel", which was adjacent to the Terminus station. These buildings on the down side were completely new – the clock tower and other structures were retained on the up side. (N. Langridge collection)

6. Another 1935 picture shows contemporary styling which was regarded by many as quite revolutionary. An important part of the previous station survived – the brick arches supporting the platforms, which can still be seen today. (N. Langridge collection)

7. The scene of devastation on no.1 platform on 22nd June 1941 was typical of what was happening in much of the rest of the city and the docks during the bombing in World War II. Some details of the 1892 building can be seen on the left. (British Rail)

8. The signal box on the left was in use from 2nd June 1935 until 8th November 1981, since when operations have been controlled from Eastleigh. No. 35015 *Rotterdam Lloyd* eases the "Bournemouth Belle" away from platform 4, whilst a Lord Nelson class 4–6–0 sizzles in the bay on 17th September 1949. (S.W. Baker)

9. Four starting signals show that up trains could depart from any platform in 1964. The steps of the public footbridge by the locomotive water tank are still formed from grey chequered paving bricks of considerable antiquity. (D. Cullum)

10. Looking from the footbridge in March 1965, we see no. 34024 *Tamar Valley*, ready to depart with a Bournemouth to York service. The platform canopies and the combined passenger and luggage bridge date from 1935 whilst the main buildings and clock tower are of 1892 origin. (E. Wilmshurst)

11. A view from above the tunnel mouth in May 1966 reveals conductor rails lying in the "four-foot" and insulators already in place. After the demolition of the power station, a geothermal energy borehole was drilled on the site, which is now occupied by a toy superstore. (D. Cullum)

12. This 1981 photograph shows a stopping train to Bournemouth passing under the much-photographed semaphore signal bridge which was redundant at the end of that year. The five storey office block on the right was built in 1968 to replace the earlier up buildings, the station offices now occupying the ground floor. (D. Fereday Glenn)

13. The brick-lined tunnel has presented stability problems for many years and in 1983-84 major remedial works were undertaken. This involved removing one track completely during the work; building a new concrete invert in stages and laying a 2ft gauge railway each side of the remaining single track, which was centrally located. Engineers worked on a movable bridge shield, cutting out the brickwork and replacing it with bolted segments. Rubble was removed on the north narrow gauge line whilst the one seen here took in ready-mixed concrete grouting. (V. Mitchell)

14. Extensive sidings were provided and up to 20 locomotives were allocated to the Docks Locomotive shed to shunt them. Four ex-LBSCR engines are to be seen at work on 3rd August 1956 and in the background is Rank's gigantic flour mill, one of several commercial premises to be erected on the reclaimed land. These generated little traffic. (E. Wilmshurst)

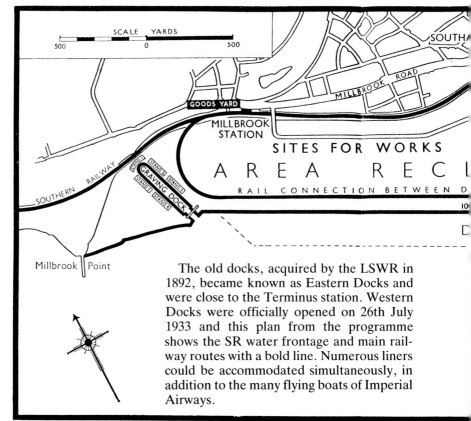

The old docks, acquired by the LSWR in 1892, became known as Eastern Docks and were close to the Terminus station. Western Docks were officially opened on 26th July 1933 and this plan from the programme shows the SR water frontage and main railway routes with a bold line. Numerous liners could be accommodated simultaneously, in addition to the many flying boats of Imperial Airways.

15. Numerous locomotives were shipped from the USA during WWII for use in Europe and after the war the SR bought a batch of these 0–6–0s, mainly for shunting in the Docks. This example is seen on 2nd July 1967, running on recessed track into one of the transit sheds – both typical features of the new docks. At the end of World War II, train ferry berths were located near Mayflower Park and the King George V Graving Dock. (S.C. Nash)

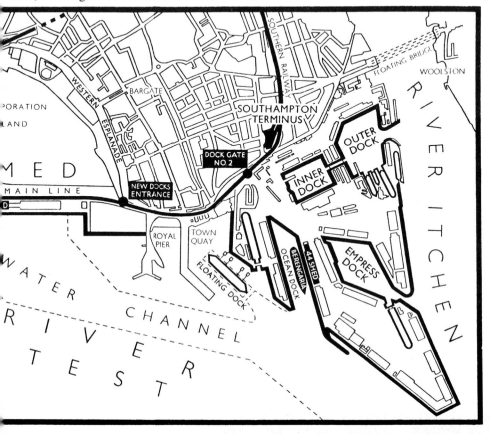

16. The first "West Country" class to be built, no. 34001 *Exeter*, is seen departing with the 10.57 Boat Train for Waterloo on 24th June 1967, the last year of steam operation in the area. A few of the 111 cranes are visible – most have now been scrapped or sold, with the advent of containerisation. (E. Wilmshurst)

MILLBROOK

18. The station was opened in November 1861 and this photograph was taken about 20 years later. We are looking east at the assort-ed timber structures, which include the plat-form faces. (National Railway Museum)

←

17. Cranage was necessary again on 23rd January 1986 when the last of four General Motors 3300HP diesel-electric locomotives arrived from USA. Another class 59 waits in the background to be moved to Foster Yeoman's stone quarry in Somerset. (D.J. Kemp)

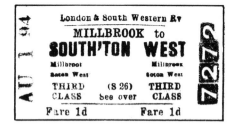

London & South Western Ry
MILLBROOK to
SOUTH'TON WEST
Millbrook   Millbrook
Soton West   Soton West
THIRD   (S 26)   THIRD
CLASS   See over   CLASS
Fare 1d   Fare 1d

7277

SOUTHERN RAILWAY.
Issued subject to the Bye-laws, Regulations &
Conditions in the Company's Bills and Notices.
Millbrook   to
Millbrook   Millbrook
Southampton Cen.   Southampton Cen.
SOUTHAMPTON CENTRAL
THIRD CLASS   THIRD CLASS
Fare 3d.   Fare 3d.
NOT TRANSFERABLE

2698

19. A westward view shows the entrance to the booking office on the left and the goods yard beyond. Corporation tramcars terminated outside the station in later years – see map. (Lens of Sutton)

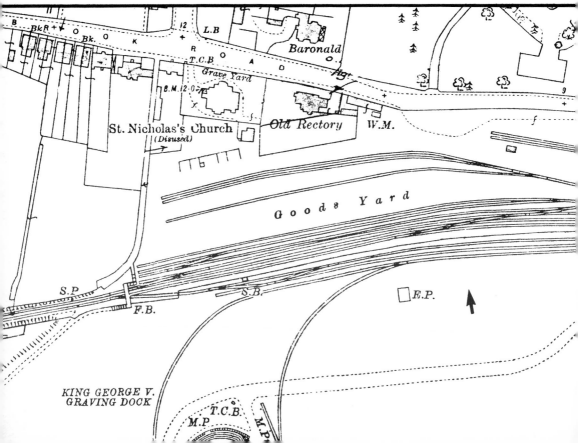

20. A new station on an island platform in the centre of the four through lines was built in 1935, as was the signal box beyond the footbridge. The two tracks in the foreground of this 1965 photograph led to the Western Docks. (C.L. Caddy)

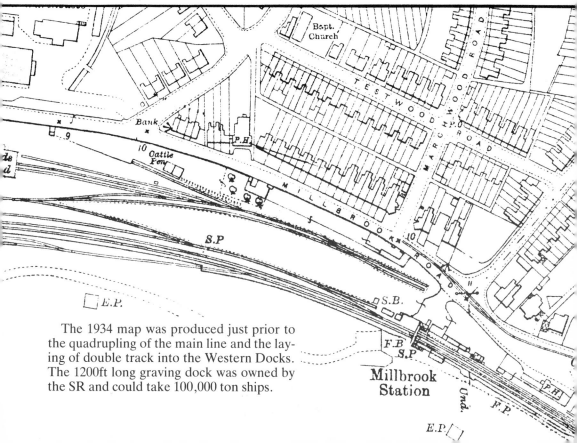

The 1934 map was produced just prior to the quadrupling of the main line and the laying of double track into the Western Docks. The 1200ft long graving dock was owned by the SR and could take 100,000 ton ships.

21. BR class 4 no. 80152 powers a stopping train to Bournemouth on 6th May 1967, in the twilight of steam operation. This station is now unstaffed and all stations west of Southampton are "open", ticket collecting being carried out on the train. (S.C. Nash)

22. The 11.05 Birmingham to Weymouth service on 15th September 1979 runs on the down through line, behind no. 33113. Local trains use the two centre tracks, either side of the platform, whilst the two on the right link the main line, near the bridge, with the GPO Terminal and the Western Docks. There is no longer a waterfront line to the Eastern Docks or a Post Office siding. (J. Scrace)

23. Millbrook Freightliner Terminal is seen here occupying the site of the goods yard which closed in July 1967. The line on the right leads to the Maritime Freightliner Terminal and the Freightliner wagon shop. The 10.10 Portsmouth Harbour to Bristol, behind no. 33062, leaves the end of the quadruple track on 27th September 1986, whilst no. 47280 *Pedigree* stands in the siding. From 1943 until 1946 there was a double track connection between Millbrook Docks and Redbridge. (D.J. Kemp)

REDBRIDGE

In 1867, Redbridge was still a small village located between the River Test and the former canal to Andover and Salisbury. The station opened with the line.

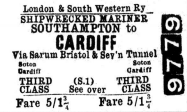

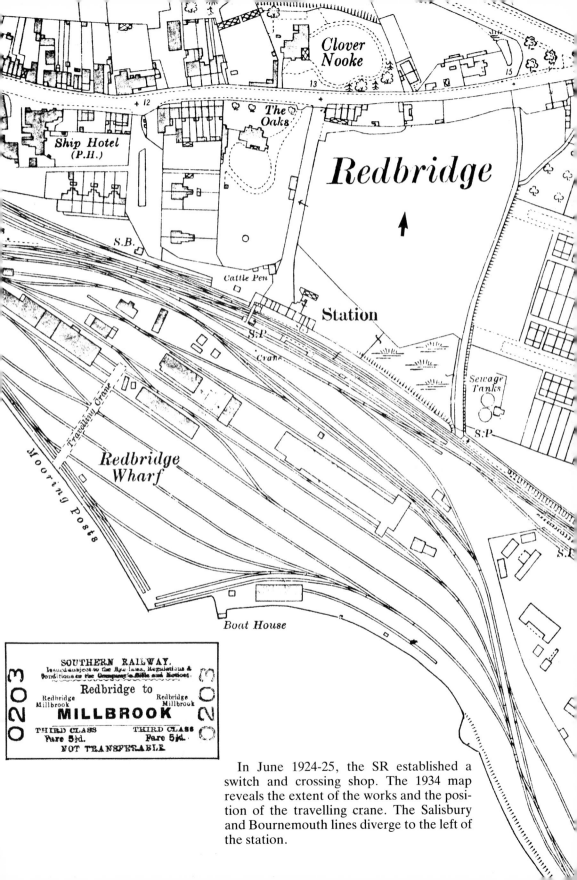

Clover Nooke

The Oaks

Ship Hotel (P.H.)

Redbridge

S.B.

Cattle Pen

Station

S.P.

Crane

Travelling Crane

Redbridge Wharf

Mooring Posts

Sewage Tanks

S.P.

S.P.

Boat House

In June 1924-25, the SR established a switch and crossing shop. The 1934 map reveals the extent of the works and the position of the travelling crane. The Salisbury and Bournemouth lines diverge to the left of the station.

24. In 1884, the LSWR established its sleeper works between the main line and wharfs that were built to receive the imported timber. Built as a 2–2–0T, class C14 no. 77S is found shunting in the works on 25th June 1939. (S.W. Baker)

25. Prior to the import of jarrah sleepers from Australia, timber was impregnated with creosote under pressure in giant autoclaves. The loads were moved on narrow gauge wagons by man power, or woman power, during WWII. (British Rail)

26. Women were also employed at that time to load scrap chairs for recasting in the works foundry into new track parts. The detailed story of the SR during WWII is told in *War on the Line*, reprinted in 1984 by Middleton Press. (British Rail)

27. A December 1945 view of part of the works includes a steam crane towing a wagon and both men and women at work. The latter were soon sent back home for good, as men returned from the war. (British Rail)

28. An up freight from Bournemouth crosses the junction with the Salisbury line on 18th May 1963. On the left is part of the machine shop, in which giant planing machines create the taper on point blades. The road to the works passed over six tracks. (E. Wilmshurst)

29. The Plymouth to Brighton service rounds the curve from Salisbury, behind class 4MT no. 75068. The cranes in the background are working on the new road bridge in 1966 and, on the right, the former cattle dock can be seen. The signal box and the connection from the works on the extreme left were taken out of use in February 1982. (D. Fereday Glenn)

30. An eastward view from the footbridge in 1973 helps to locate the present foundry in the right background. It has subsequently been fitted with taller dust separating chimneys and consumes about five tons of casting sand (from Redhill) per week to produce 55 tons of track components. (D. Cullum)

31. The small station buildings are now obscured from most angles. The complex footbridge replaced a simple SR concrete structure and enables staff to reach the works in greater safety. The works equipment includes a modern rail welding plant – butt welds being now possible in under two minutes per join. (V. Mitchell)

32. A new viaduct over the River Test was completed in 1964 and the tracks were slewed into position on 30th May. We look towards Redbridge as the work is nearing completion. (J.H. Bird)

33. West of the viaduct, a causeway extends towards Totton. A Bromford Bridge to Fawley empty oil train is seen running onto it on 6th November 1965, hauled by no. D6524. The old road bridge can be picked out between the cranes constructing the new one. (E. Wilmshurst)

TOTTON

34. The first station was known as Eling Junction until 1859 although no passenger service was provided to Eling, a village of some antiquity ½ mile to the south. The single platform was near to the later goods shed. A train from Southampton is shown passing over the level crossing which was closed in 1930, along with the associated signal box which is obscured by the engine. (Lens of Sutton)

35. Looking west from the footbridge seen in the previous view, we see Peter Mumford & Sons 1885 Flour Mills, which had their own private siding until 1965. The down platform now only has a small glass shelter but the up buildings are retained in good order, with a manned booking office. (Lens of Sutton)

36. An enthusiasts railtour stands on the up line on 19th March 1966, while visitors examine the northern part of the Eling Tramway on the right. The splitting signals by the class Q1 are for the Fawley branch and Totton goods yard. (S.C. Nash)

37. The signal box at Junction Road controlled crossing gates as well as the junctions and was built on top of the former crossing keeper's cottage – hence the unusual windows. It was known as Eling Junction until February 1950 and was closed on 28th February 1982. The photograph was taken in February 1968 and lifting barriers were installed in 1974. (J. Scrace)

38. The high gabled station dates from 1859 and is seen here in 1974, some time after the original entrance had been blocked up and a letter box built into the brickwork. The wooden building on the right had been the station master's office for many years. (J. Scrace)

39. No. 73004 heads the 9.36 Waterloo to Weymouth Quay train on 22nd July 1978 and passes the Fawley branch and loop. Four sidings were retained for the storage of oil trains and the reversal of empty tankers for Furzebrook. Tankers loaded with crude oil from Britain's largest onshore oil field at Wytch Farm reverse at Redbridge – see our *Branch Line to Swanage* for details of this traffic. The goods yard closed on 2nd October 1967, the shed being demolished in March 1987. (J. Scrace)

St. Mary's Hall

Forest Lodge

Saw Mills

S.P

Cr.

W.M.

Goods Shed

F.B.

S.B.

JUNCTION ROAD

Brokenford Lane

OSBORNE

BROKENFORD AVE.

BROKENFORD AVENUE

Club

Hall

RUM BRIDGE STREET

Sunday School

Cinema

WINSOR ROAD

BARTRAM ROAD

FISHER ROAD

ROSE ROAD

Inf't Sch

SCHOOL ROAD

ELING TRAMWAY

The Eling branch was built by the South-ampton and Dorchester Railway, largely on private land. It was a freight only line serving a tar distillery, chemical works, corn mill, saw mill and the waterfront wharves. This 1933 edition shows the northern part of the half-mile long branch.

40. A northward view on 17th February 1987 shows no. 56031 *Merehead* running round its train of four-wheeled hopper wagons, which was conveying roadstone from Somerset to the ARC coating plant, seen on the left. This was then the only traffic on the branch, the train arriving at 11.35, up to three times a week. (N. Stanyon)

41. Looking south in 1982, a siding can be seen curving away sharply behind the crane, into the saw mills. On the right are narrow gauge lines running into the cylindrical autoclave, used for pressure creosoting of timber. South Western Tar Distillers' sidings were last used for the despatch of bitumen, having earlier received tar from such places as Aldershot and Reading. (J.R. Fairman)

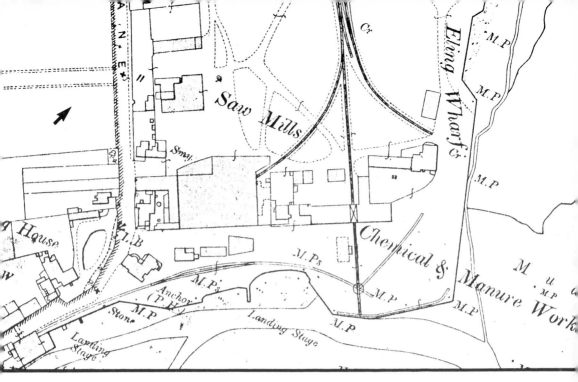

The southern end of the branch is shown on the 1909 edition. In 1987, track was still visible on the wharf near the flour mill, which has been restored to working order. It operates on tidal power and is open to the public.

42. Another 1982 photograph shows the *MV Sea Skerry* at Eling Wharf and the grid cables from Marchwood Power Station. Goods inward has included Scandinavian timber, ballast and tar from coastal gas works, such as Poole. (J.R. Fairman)

FAWLEY BRANCH
MARCHWOOD

43. No less than five level crossings preceded the one from which this photograph was taken in 1952. Most have subsequently received automatic half barriers but here gates were still opened manually in 1987. The branch to the Military Port diverges beyond the end of the platform, having been opened on 28th November 1943. (D. Cullum)

44. A passing loop was opened in June 1960 to accommodate the heavy oil train traffic that was developing. The operating problems were eased by the withdrawal of passenger services on 14th February 1966, a week after this photograph was taken. DEMUs started to replace steam-hauled services in 1961. Look for the signalman's mirror.
(D. Fereday Glenn)

45. Empty oil tanks approach from Totton as the signalman opens the gates by hand in 1982. He jumps back into the electronic age on returning to his box, to observe the TV screen which is coupled to Eastleigh Panel. It shows the main line and trains arriving for the branch. (J.R. Fairman)

46. The loop was signalled for reversible running and has a curious kink in it resulting from the incorporation of a former siding and the position of the station buildings. No. 33059 moves north loaded with aviation spirit bound for Salfords near Gatwick Airport, on 5th March 1982. (J.S. Petley)

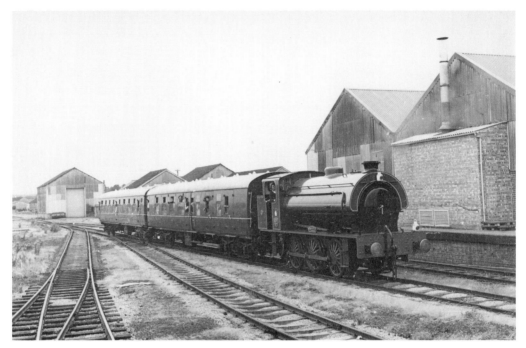

47. The Marchwood Military Port was a scene of great activity in 1944 at the time of the Normandy landings as it specialises in waterfront equipment. The Army's 0–6–0ST *Waggoner* was involved in recreational activity when photographed at an Open Day on 22nd July 1978. (J. Scrace)

48. On 21st July 1979, a Western Region DMU arrived with a party of railway enthusiasts for another open day. The Army diesel locomotive is no. AD432, built by Ruston Hornsby. (S.C. Nash)

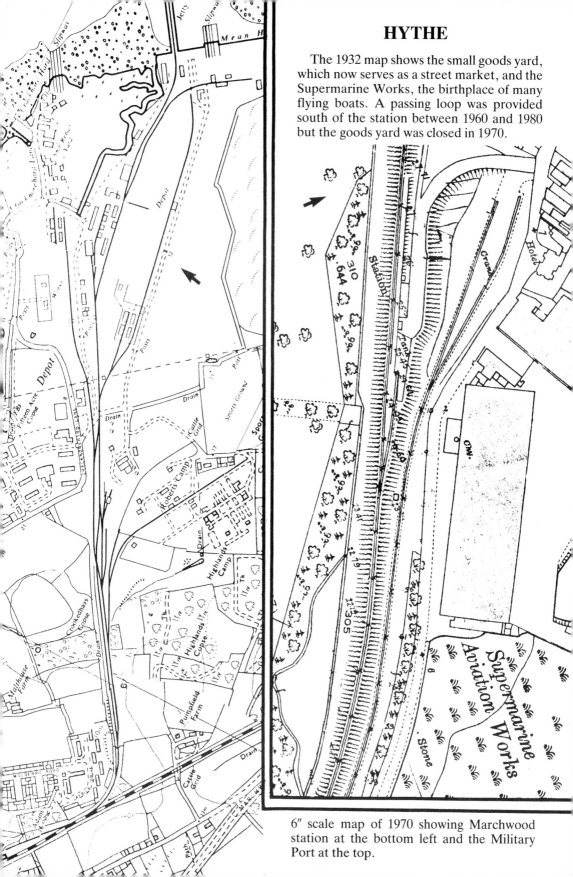

HYTHE

The 1932 map shows the small goods yard, which now serves as a street market, and the Supermarine Works, the birthplace of many flying boats. A passing loop was provided south of the station between 1960 and 1980 but the goods yard was closed in 1970.

6″ scale map of 1970 showing Marchwood station at the bottom left and the Military Port at the top.

49. Unlike Marchwood, Hythe was provided with electric lighting from the outset, the current being supplied by the Hythe Pier Tramway. This is the first train arriving from Fawley, without special ceremony, on 20th July 1925. (Lens of Sutton)

50. All three stations on the branch were of similar design and were all finished with pebble-dashed rendering, so popular in the 1920s. Class M7 no. 30032 waits to depart for Fawley on 11th June 1959. It might call at Hardley which was a halt in use from 1958 to 1965. (A.E. Bennett)

51. Hythe's first railway was laid along the pier in 1909 by Mr. Kingham, the local undertaker, the pier itself having been completed in 1880. The two-foot gauge train is seen leaving the pier head on 9th September 1949. Electrification at 110 volts DC took place in 1922, using a third rail conductor and three locomotives built by Brush. (S.W. Baker)

52. At the shore end, a siding is provided to the workshop and another accommodates a locomotive and tank wagon which takes diesel oil to the ferry boat. The filler pipe is seen on the left. The three bogie passenger cars were built by Drewry and each seated about 48 people. (S.C. Nash)

FAWLEY

53. A busy scene, photographed in June 1959, eight years after the giant Esso refinery transformed the area, shows class M7 no. 30032 taking water and the fireman damping down the coal dust in its bunker. (A.E. Bennett)

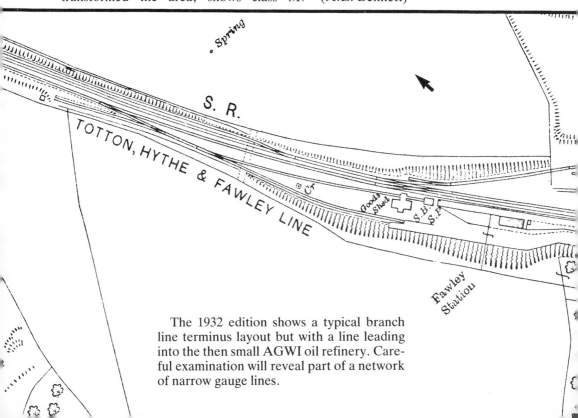

The 1932 edition shows a typical branch line terminus layout but with a line leading into the then small AGWI oil refinery. Careful examination will reveal part of a network of narrow gauge lines.

54. The signal box, like the one at Hampton Court Junction, was one of the few built by the SR to a traditional design instead of their more universal flat-roofed Odeon style. The inclined approach to the station from Marsh Lane can be seen in the background of this 1964 picture. On the left is an ex-GWR water tank, removed from Warminster. (C.L. Caddy)

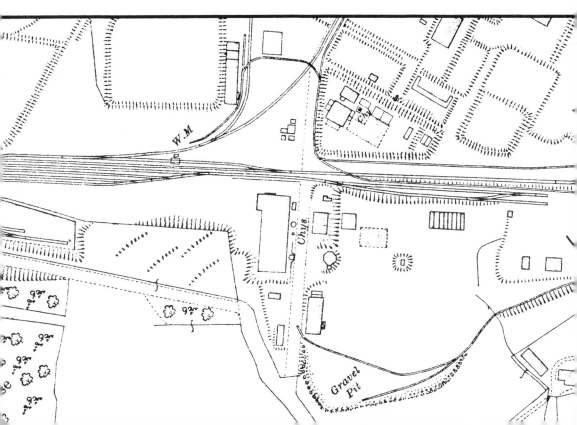

55. Two views taken in 1970 give an indication of the forest of chimneys and tanks that now surround the railway. No. 6539 departs for Wolverhampton on 22nd July and runs past the former local goods shed which was closed in 1967. Other private sidings served Union Carbide Ltd. and the International Synthetic Rubber Co. – now Enoxy Chemicals. (J. Scrace)

56. No. 6537 arrives from Bromford Bridge, near Birmingham on the same day. The entire station area has now been incorporated into the Esso plant and is therefore no longer accessible. The station has been demolished and the signal box was closed in 1978, the line up to Marchwood being operated on the Key Token system. (J. Scrace)

LYNDHURST ROAD

57. The station opened with the line and served the nearby village of Ashurst, Lyndhurst being 2½ miles distant. Here we see Ground Frame A and the small goods dock in 1952. Ground Frame B was further south and controlled entry to a long siding on the down side. (D. Cullum)

The 1933 map shows the road bridge that had been opened in August 1932 to replace the level crossing. The station was unusual in having single sidings at all four points of the compass. They ceased to be used in 1964-65, having earlier despatched a heavy traffic in timber.

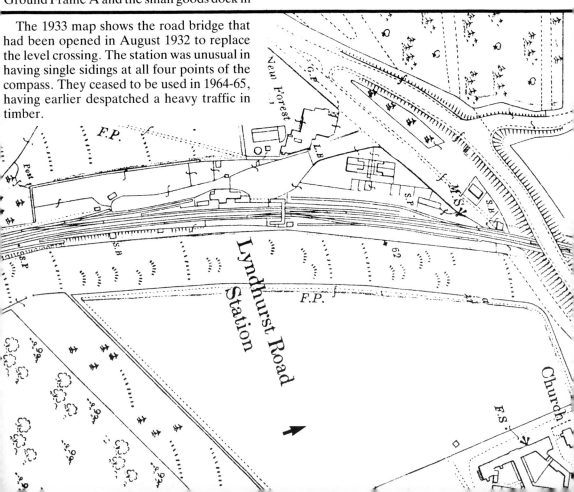

58. No. 34025 *Whimple* heads a LCGB special train from Lymington to Waterloo on 9th April 1967, the locomotive being on the site of the former level crossing. The station house is extant but only small glass shelters exist for passengers. The covered footbridge has been replaced by a simple steel structure and the signal box was closed in October 1966. Partly obscured by smoke is the bus garage which housed two vehicles used on the unsuccessful service to Lyndhurst in 1904-05. (E. Wilmshurst)

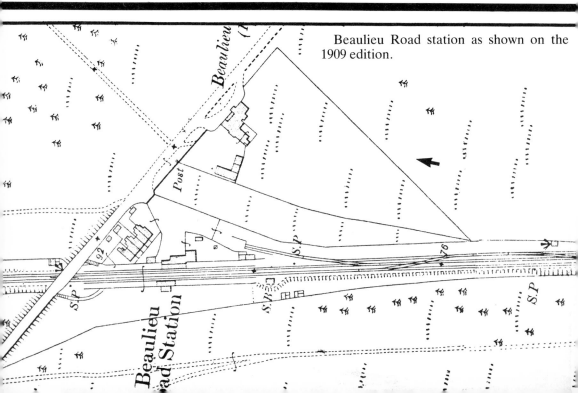

Beaulieu Road station as shown on the 1909 edition.

BEAULIEU ROAD

59. This remote station is over three miles from the nearest village. Although it opened with the line, it was closed between 1860 and 1895 and can never have been a great traffic centre. The single siding on the left was once busy after the nearby pony sales but it closed in 1960. The signal box is beyond the up platform canopy and was last used in 1933.
(D. Cullum collection)

60. Looking north in 1964, the year in which the station ceased to be staffed, it is evident that passengers had to cross the line by means of the road bridge. The station is on the first twist in Castleman's corkscrew which placed it so far from habitation. The area is still devoid of mains electricity, the station lighting being taken from the railway supply.
(C.L. Caddy)

BROCKENHURST

61. An early postcard shows East Box which superseded the crossing keeper, whose cottage is adjacent. In the centre is the smithy shop, often an important requisite for the traveller with a defective horseshoe. (D. Cullum collection)

The 1867 map shows the station to be an unexpected distance from the main road. It also shows the pound, close to the smithy, where stray animals would be placed.

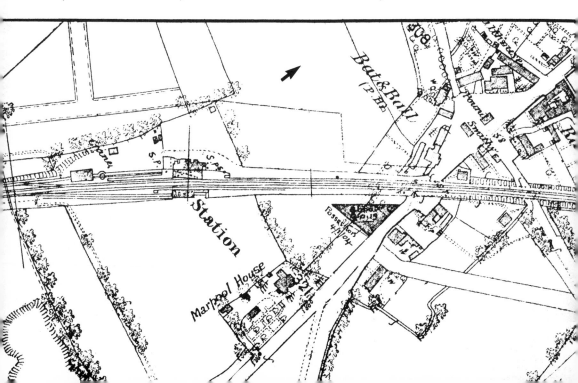

62. Until the station was rebuilt in 1936, the platform on the right was the down bay for branch trains. The line was then extended to form a loop, resulting in two island platforms being available. (Lens of Sutton)

63. The bridge over the dock and goods road is visible on the left whilst branch line trains are seen in both loop lines. Services from Lymington and Ringwood mostly terminated here. (D. Cullum collection)

64. The new profile of the canopy extension and SR lights are features of this charming picture which captures the atmosphere of a pre-war summer Saturday. The precise date is 4th September 1937 and class M7 no. 104 is working the Lymington branch service. (S.W. Baker)

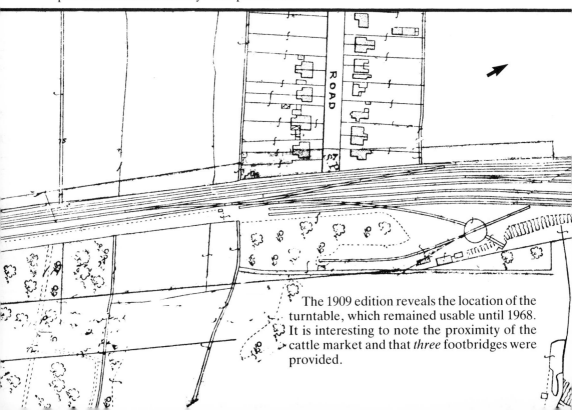

The 1909 edition reveals the location of the turntable, which remained usable until 1968. It is interesting to note the proximity of the cattle market and that *three* footbridges were provided.

65. Little has changed since this picture was taken in 1966, except that the land is now used as a "car parking facility" (formerly known as a car park). Even the delightful no.8 crossing cottage in the distance still displays its fine polychromatic brickwork. In 1987, the goods shed housed a firm supplying wood-burning heaters. (D. Cullum)

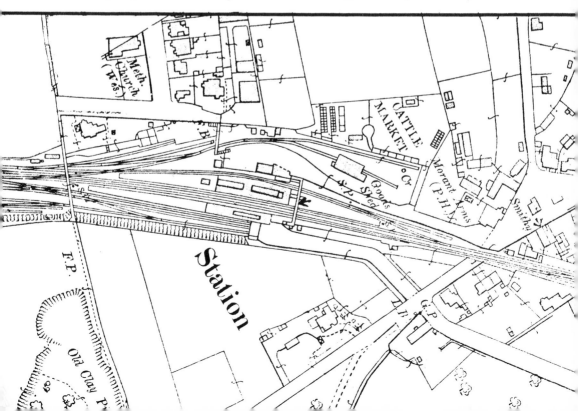

66. The last day of steam working of the Lymington branch was recorded on 30th March 1967, as no. 80146 runs into the up loop. Engineer's equipment stands at the former cattle dock and the West Box is just visible in the distance. A private siding for the British Oxygen Co. was opened in 1986. (J. Scrace)

67. DEMUs were used briefly on the branch but 2-coach EMUs have subsequently provided most of the services, with eight coaches from Waterloo appearing on summer Saturdays. The four down sidings appear busy in this August 1969 photograph – there were seven more longer sidings beyond these. (D. Cullum)

68. An unusual feature of the up loop is the luggage platform which is interlocked to the signalling panel and also carries a red lamp, seen here mounted on a pole. The white shed was a cycle store and the building beyond it was used as a staff room. (J. Scrace)

69. East Box was replaced by this one in November 1964 when the lifting barriers came into use. The lever frame was replaced by a signalling panel on 19th October 1978 and West Box was closed, together with many others. The panel now controls from Totton to Hinton Admiral on the down line; Christchurch to Lyndhurst Road on the up and also the Lymington branch. The entrance to the short-lived Motorail Terminal to Stirling is shown in 1976. (J. Scrace)

LYMINGTON JCT

30052

40

S.W.R.

1909 edition

DORCHESTER

S.Ps

Lymington Junction

4ft.R.H.

S.P.

4ft.R.H.

70. Class M7 no. 30052 leaves the Lymington branch at Lymington Junction, one mile south of Brockenhurst, on 18th April 1964. On the right, the lines to Ringwood curve away from the present line. That part of Castleman's famous corkscrew route to Dorchester ceased to carry passengers on 4th May 1964 and closed totally on 30th March 1965. (E. Wilmshurst)

71. No. 34089. "Battle of Britain" class *602 Squadron*, speeds over the junction, bound for Weymouth on 1st April 1967. The single line tablet catcher is silhouetted against the box. The latter closed when Brockenhurst panel came into use and, at the same time, an independent third track, parallel to the main line, became available for branch trains. (C.L. Caddy)

September 1964

SOUTHAMPTON, TOTTON and FAWLEY

Miles																										
		Mondays to Fridays only																								
		am				pm																				
	LONDON Waterloo 32 dep	2 45	..	..	..	1 30	..	..	..	..	..	..	..	..	..	..	..	..	..	..	..	..	..	..	..	..
—	Southampton Terminus. dep	....				....																			
1¾	Southampton Central.. ,,	6 43	..	..	..	3 58	..	..	..	..	..	..	..	..	..	..	..	..	..	..	..	..	..	..	..
2¼	Millbrook	6 45				4 2																			
4¼	Redbridge	6 49				4 5																			
5	Totton	6 53				4 10																			
8¼	Marchwood	7 5				4 21																			
11½	Hythe	7 15				4 30																			
14½	Fawley .. .. .. arr	7 26	..		..	4 39	..																		
		Mondays to Fridays only																								
Miles		am		pm																					
	Fawley .. .. dep	8 6	..	4 48	..	..	..	..	..	..	..	..	..	..	..	..	..	..	..	..	..	..	..	..	..
3	Hythe	8 15		4 57																					
6	Marchwood	8 24		5 6																					
9¼	Totton	8 36		5 18																					
10¼	Redbridge	8 38		5 21																					
12	Millbrook	8 42		5 25																					
12¾	Southampton Central.. arr	8 46		5 27																					
14½	Southampton Terminus. ,,	....		....																					
92	LONDON Waterloo 32 arr	1050	..	8 15																					

LYMINGTON BRANCH
AMPRESS WORKS HALT

72. A private halt, south of the A337 road bridge, was opened on the east side of the line for the use of employees of Wellworthy, manufacturers of piston rings. It came into use on 1st October 1956 and, in 1987, one train per day each way normally stopped there. A halt at Shirley Holmes, 1½ miles south of the junction, had been in use in the late 19th century. (C.L. Caddy)

2nd · SINGLE   SINGLE · 2nd

0827

Lymington Town to
Lymington Town   Lymington Town

Ampress Works H't   Ampress Works H't
AMPRESS WORKS HALT

.S, 3d.   FARE 3d (S)

0827

For conditions see over For conditions see over

SOUTHAMPTON, TOTTON, and FAWLEY.—Week Days only.

Mls		mrn		aft	aft	8 X	aft	Mls		mrn	8 X		aft	aft	aft
	London (Waterloo) K 324 dep	...	...	8 X	*2 35	3 30	3 30	3	Fawley (Hants)..............dep	8 6	1155		1212	5 19	6 43
—	Southampton Terminus dep	...	...			5 3|	5 38	3	Hythe (Hants).................	8 14	12 3		1229	5 27	6 51
1½	Southampton Central ... "	6 57	...	4 11	5 38	5 44		6	Marchwood	8 25	1213		1229	5 38	7 1
2½	Millbrook........................	7 2	...		5 42			9½	Totton L 324	8 37	1225		1241	5 51	7 13
4½	Redbridge.......................	7 7	...		5 48			10½	Redbridge 375................	8 40	...		1243	5 54	7 16
5	Totton L........................	7 10	...	4 2	4 19	5 51	5 51	12	Millbrook...............[524	8 44	...		1247	6 0	7 20
8½	Marchwood.....................	7 22	...	4 11	4 29	6 2	6 2	12½	Southampton Cen. 330, arr.	8 48	...		1251	6 4	7 24
11½	Hythe (Hants).................	7 32	...	4 21	4 39	6 12	6 12	14½	Southampton G 524.... "	8 55	...		...	...	7 31
14	Fawley (Hants)...........arr.	7 43	...	4 31	4 49	6 22	6 22	94	London (Waterloo) K 330 arr	1030	...		2 39	8 15	10Y39

G Southampton Terminus (for Docks).   K Via Southampton Central.   L Station for Eling.
8 X or SX Saturdays excepted.   Y Arr. 10 23 aft. on Sats. until 3rd Sept.

Fawley branch – July 1938

LYMINGTON TOWN

73. An Edwardian postcard gives an impression of the splendid brickwork and the varied road transport of the period. The station was meticulously restored in 1986 by BR and local organisations, a booking office being retained but much of the building being let for office use. Although the branch opened on 12th July 1858, this terminus was not ready until 19th September 1860!
(Lens of Sutton)

Map date - 1932. The temporary terminus was a wooden building close to Bridge Road level crossing and survived until 1954.

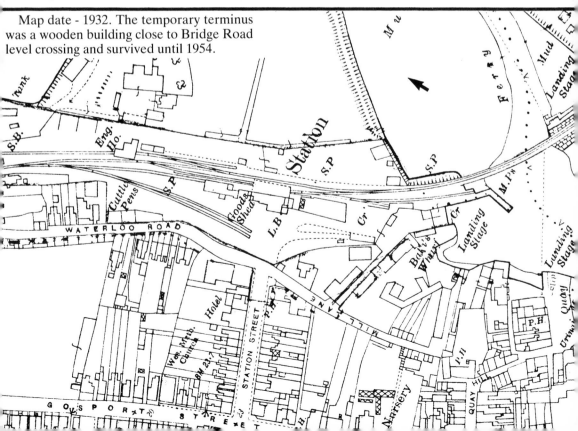

74. The signal box, seen in the distance, controlled the gates at Bridge Road and was opened in 1928, replacing one opposite the station buildings. It was closed in 1979 when lifting barriers came into use, controlled under CCTV from Brockenhurst. The sidings and engine shed road ceased to be used on 3rd April 1967, just after this photograph was taken. (C.L. Caddy)

LONDON, BROCKENHURST, and LYMINGTON.

(Timetable — Week Days, Down and Up; Sundays, Down and Up. Detailed train times shown in original.)

Down. — Week Days.

Miles from Brockenhurst				
Waterloo 324 .... dep.				
Southampton Cent. 324 "				
Brockenhurst .... dep.				
Lymington Town B. ...... "				
" Pier ...... arr.				

Up. — Week Days.

Lymington Pier ...... dep.			
" Town B. ... "			
Brockenhurst 324 .... arr.			
Southampton Cent. 330 arr.			
Waterloo 330 .... "			

Down. — Sundays.

Waterloo 324 .... dep.				
Southampton Cent. 324 "				
Brockenhurst .... dep.				
Lymington Town B. .... arr.				
" Pier ...... "				

Up. — Sundays.

Lymington Pier ...... dep.			
" Tn. B. ... "			
Brockenhurst 324 .... arr.			
Southampton C. 330 arr.			
Waterloo 330 .... "			

a 2 minutes later on Sats. **B** Sta. for Milford-on-Sea (3¾ miles). Omnibus Service available by Hants and Dorset Motor Services Ltd. **C** By Bus. **D** Restaurant Car provided until 3rd Sept. only. d Mons. to Fris. until 2nd Sept., Fridays only thereafter. **F** On 17th and 24th Sept. only. **H** Sats. only. Not after 10th Sept. h 4 mins. earlier on Sats. **L** or L Sats. only. Not after 3rd Sept. **N** Restaurant Car to and from Lymington Pier. **P** Pullman Car Train. 1st and 3rd class Pullman Cars between London (W.) and Southampton Central. Supplementary Fees Charged. **R** Restaurant Car between London and Southampton Cen. **S O** or **SO** Saturdays only. **S X** or **SX** Saturdays excepted. **T** Restaurant Car between London and Brockenhurst. t Arr. Waterloo 10 36 aft. commencing 10th Sept. u Dep. 12 25 aft. on Tues. and Weds. to 14th Sept.; also on 21st Sept. **V** Restaurant Car between Waterloo and Brockenhurst provided on Sats. until 3rd Sept. **W** Restaurant Car between Southampton Central and Waterloo on Sats. until 3rd Sept. only. **WSO** Weds. and Sats.

1938

75. The overall roof was partly destroyed by enemy bombs in 1941 and over 25 years later it was demolished, together with the goods shed on the right. (C.L. Caddy)

76. The siding in the centre of the picture passes the cattle dock and originally extended to a jetty built by the LSWR in 1861 for the Isle of Wight ferries. The mud banks and bends in the River Lymington made this a very unsatisfactory terminal point and so the railway was extended to a new pier on 1st May 1884. The line is seen curving away to the left to reach the bridge over the river. (Lens of Sutton)

77. Lymington town public slip and landing stage is in front of the paddle steamer and the unsuccessful railway jetty is behind it. Town station is at the right of the picture. (Lens of Sutton)

78. The LSWR was not required to provide the great headroom under its bridge that many railways were forced to make at river crossings. This was due to the shallow water limiting the draught of vessels and thus the navigation potential. BR standard class 4 tank no. 80152 wends its way back to Brockenhurst on 1st April 1967. (C.L. Caddy)

LYMINGTON PIER

79. The LSWR acquired the ferry service to Yarmouth in July 1884, two months after this station came into use. Passengers had the convenience of cross platform transfer between ship and train. The railway tunnel to Yarmouth, proposed prior to World War I, would have been even more convenient. (D. Cullum collection)

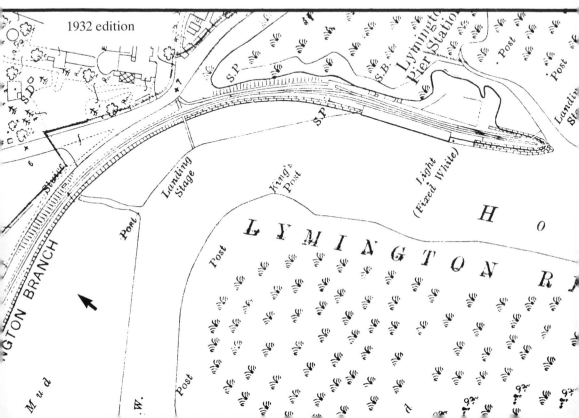

1932 edition

are given on another page.
was superseded by a new
further in
(E.F. Bishop photograph).

80. Looking inland in 1950, the cattle pens are evident beyond the signal box. The latter was superseded by a flat-roofed building, further north, on 11th November 1956. (E.R. Lacey collection)

82. In 1938, a slipway was constructed to enable end-loading vehicle ferries to be introduced. The canopy was reconstructed, with a wall to reduce draughts, and a level crossing provided for access to the slipway. The siding, known as the trestle road, was added at the same time. Class Q1 stands at the head of the Waterloo train, as passengers disembark from the *Freshwater* on 23rd July 1960. (D. Fereday Glenn)

81. The replacement signal box, seen in the background, was in turn closed in March 1968 and was still standing in 1987, serving as a marine store. Class M7 no. 30029 departs at 4.35pm on 5th September 1959. (S.C. Nash)

83. Another 1960 photograph shows the unusual arrangement of crossing gates. The previous picture was taken from the other side of the signal. A new car ferry terminal was opened on the other side of the station in 1976, making this crossing almost redundant. It is now only used in emergencies. (D. Fereday Glenn)

84. One of BR's popular 'Standard 4s' stands at the end of the road on 25th June 1966, waiting to run round its train. The outline of the Isle of Wight is visible in the distance. (E. Wilmshurst)

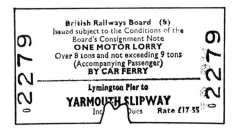

British Railways Board (S)
Issued subject to the Conditions of the
Board's Consignment Note
ONE MOTOR LORRY
Over 8 tons and not exceeding 9 tons
(Accompanying Passenger)
BY CAR FERRY
Lymington Pier to
YARMOUTH SLIPWAY
Inc   Dues   Rate £17·55

0 2279   0 2279

85. In the spring of 1986, the booking office and platform canopy were demolished. Railway passengers now leave the exposed platform at the *south* end, cross the road to the link span and gain access to the ferry via the covered way on the left. The passage has celebrated its 150th anniversary in June 1980 and is now regrettably no longer part of the railway network. (D. Fereday Glenn)

SWAY

86. Sway was the first of three intermediate stations to be opened on 6th March 1888, when the direct link between Brockenhurst and Christchurch came into use. The main buildings are on the up side, although there is a road approach to both sides. (Lens of Sutton)

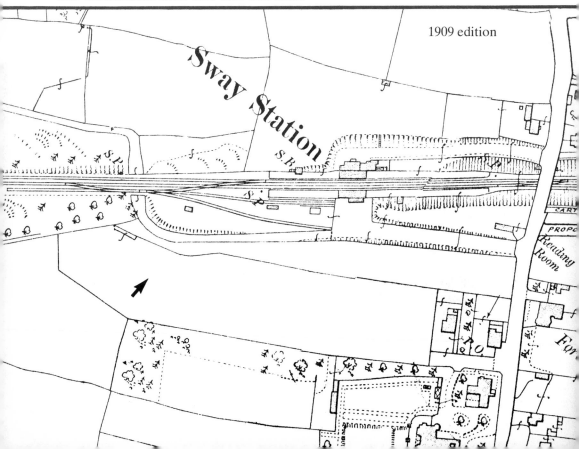

1909 edition

87. The signal box and two sidings were located at the down end of the station. The former closed in February 1967 – the latter about two years earlier. The 8.45 Weymouth to Eastleigh freight is approaching on 1st May 1965, headed by D6526. In 1948, an earth slip on Sway Bank necessitated single line working for two months, a temporary signal box being erected at Arnewood. (C.L. Caddy)

88. A Weymouth to Crewe empty pigeon special advances towards the up starting signal on 23rd May 1966, with one of the two slopes down to the station on the right. The station staff at Weymouth will have released the homing pigeons and recorded their time of departure. (J. Scrace)

89. The station house and booking office are similar to those at Swanwick and Worplesdon, all having been built in the same decade. The date over the door is AD1886 – two years *before* the opening, the reverse of events at Lymington Town. (C. Hall)

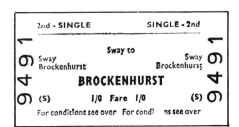

90. The layout, architecture and road app-
roaches are very similar to those at Sway but
the district has been subject to greater urban
development. Barton-on-Sea is less than two
miles away and contributes some passenger
traffic. (Lens of Sutton)

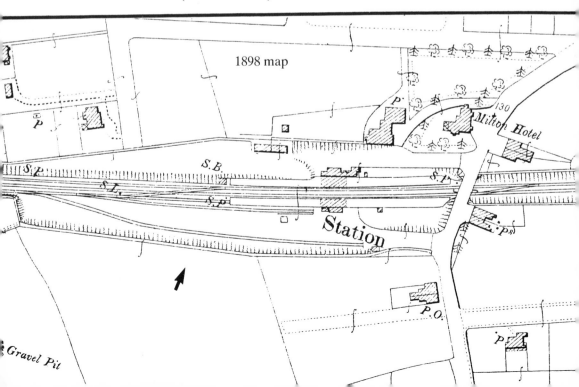

91. Another early postcard shows the station to be the nucleus around which house building commenced. This photograph was taken from the top of the castellated tower seen in the previous one. It houses a water tank belonging to the West Hants Water Co. (Lens of Sutton)

92. SR no. 152 is one of Drummonds class K10 locomotives, intended for express passenger work but seen here reversing into New Milton goods yard to collect some wagons and its brake van. (Lens of Sutton)

93. The west end of the station is seen in June 1966, six months before the goods yard was closed and eight months before the signal box shut. The goods shed was clad with corrugated iron but the canopy over the siding had a traditional ornate valance. (J. Scrace)

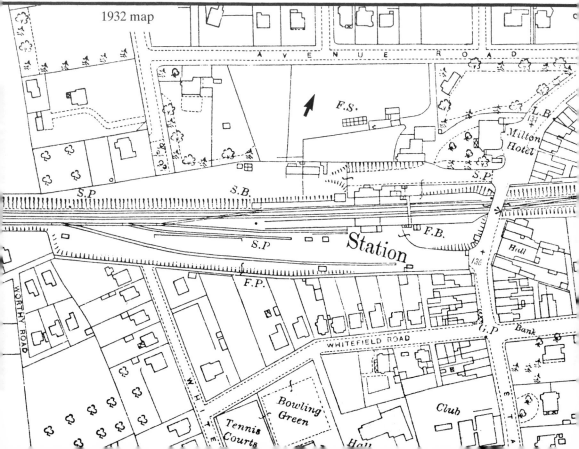

HINTON ADMIRAL

94. Until the 1950s the station had a rural location, surrounded largely by heathland and woodland. The area between the railway and the coast, one mile away, is now occupied by the residential area of Highcliffe. The dummy dormer window helps to illuminate the booking hall. (C. Hall)

95. The similarity of features of the three stations on this section of the route must have presented problems to the occasional traveller in the early part of WWII, when all station nameboards were removed. The signal box and sidings were removed in 1965-68. (C.L. Caddy)

96. The down side of all the stations of this style were provided with substantial wooden framed shelters, with corrugated iron roofs, ornate cast stanchion brackets and internal wooden benches. Not all had the added luxury of a waiting room, but all remain largely intact in 1987. (C. Hall)

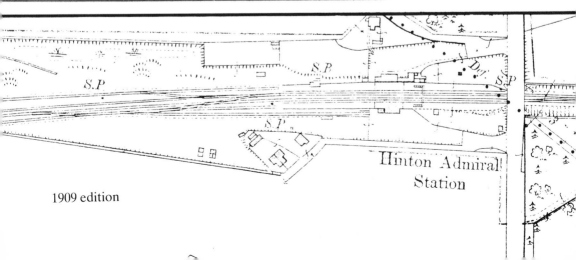

S.P

S.P

S.P

S.P

Hinton Admiral
Station

1909 edition

97. A 1963 photograph shows the remaining part of the old route from Ringwood on the left and part of the original terminus in the centre. On the right is the main line from Hinton Admiral and the five span bridge over the River Avon. (C.L. Caddy)

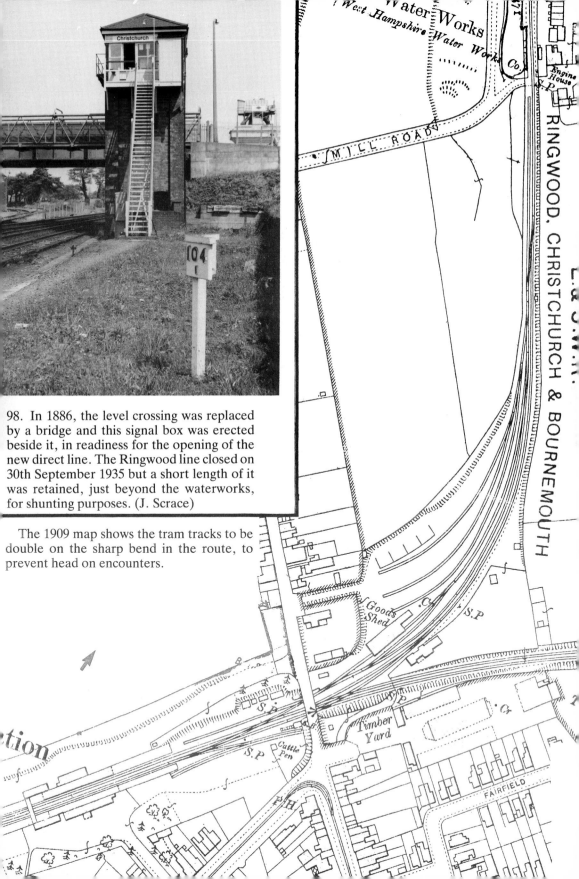

98. In 1886, the level crossing was replaced by a bridge and this signal box was erected beside it, in readiness for the opening of the new direct line. The Ringwood line closed on 30th September 1935 but a short length of it was retained, just beyond the waterworks, for shunting purposes. (J. Scrace)

The 1909 map shows the tram tracks to be double on the sharp bend in the route, to prevent head on encounters.

99. Looking west from the signal box on 24th July 1972, we witness the passage of the Bournemouth to Eastleigh freight, in the charge of E6102. The box closed on 3rd December 1972 when a ground frame, on the other side of the track, was installed to control access to the remaining sidings. These were reduced in 1973 and eliminated in 1978. (J. Scrace)

100. The south facade was photographed on the same day. The buildings had replaced the earlier ones in the summer of 1886, at the time of the doubling of the track to Bournemouth. (J. Scrace)

POKESDOWN

101. The station was opened as "Boscombe", with a single island platform, on 1st July 1886. In 1891, it was renamed "Pokesdown (Boscombe)", the suffix being dropped when Boscombe station opened in 1897. In 1930-31, the station was rebuilt with quadruple track and two outer platforms. (Lens of Sutton)

The 1933 map reveals that many of the important things in life were built close to a new railway station – the laundry, the Methodist Church, the Technical School, the Tramway Depot, an inn and the lavatories.

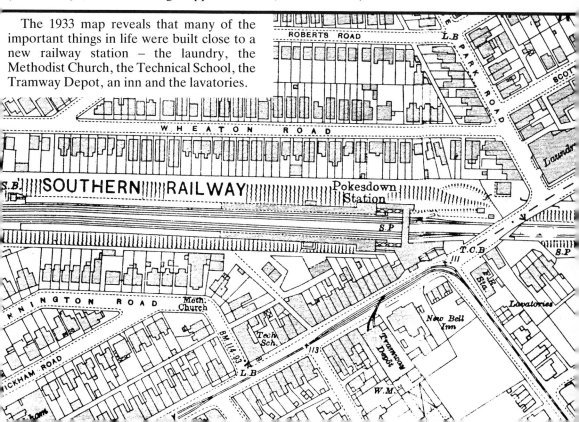

102. A transitional picture shows the new steel framed canopies nearly complete and a temporary island platform. Unfortunately the steel fascias are prone to rust and create an air of dereliction. (Lens of Sutton)

103. The new Southern Railway image was evident in the external styling – a rare phenomenon west of Southampton. The poles supported the tramway overhead equipment. (N. Langridge collection)

104. Quadruple track here gave the Operating Department a passing facility additional to the only other one on the route, at Brockenhurst. This was of particular value when holiday and residential traffic was increasing and steam services were somehwat ponderous, particularly freight. (C.L. Caddy)

105. No. 44710 was one of the class 5s introduced by the LMS in 1934 and is seen here at the head of the 11.20 Bournemouth to Newcastle service on 2nd July 1966. Four tracks were not required for the electric timetable and so the through ones were eliminated in 1971-72, along with the signal box. The latter was unusual in being entirely of steel construction. (E. Wilmshurst)

BOSCOMBE

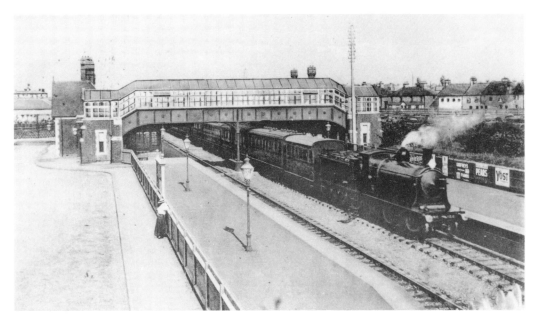

106. Opened on 1st June 1897, this is the only station on the route to have closed; for passengers on 4th October 1967 and for goods on 1st May 1972. The LSWR seems almost to have had a new architectural style for each decade. An almost identical building was opened a month earlier at Farncombe and is still largely intact. (Lens of Sutton)

107. Steam railcar no.3 was in use from 1905 to 1919 and is seen here entering the up platform. These cars mainly operated between Christchurch and Poole, being the LSWR's answer to the competition offered by the electric tramways. (Lens of Sutton)

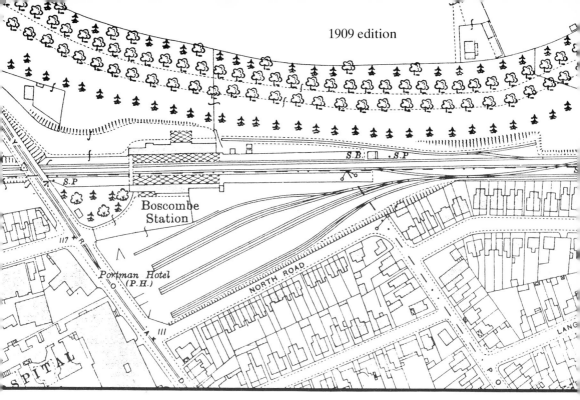

108. A Drummond class S11, no. 400, stands at the up platform blowing off beside the elegant stone-mullioned windows of this much lamented station. Only a coal yard remains as evidence of its location. (J.A.G. Coltas)

109. A westward view in 1963 illustrates the passenger comforts offered by later railway architects, such as glazed wind shields at the end of the canopies and a totally enclosed footbridge. The chimneys were fit for a country mansion. On the right is the former Carter Paterson Depot which was served by local goods trains – containers on flat wagons are visible. (C.L. Caddy)

The 1924 map shows the eastern half of the goods yard and its relationship to the signal box (S.B.) and the tramway depot. The other half of the yard is shown on the 1898 map. The entire former railway area is occupied by a business park but the tram depot remains standing.

110. Bournemouth Central Goods Box was opposite the eastern part of the yard and it functioned only as a ground frame after December 1966. The yard closed in 1979 and the box was demolished in 1986. Passing it on 23rd June 1970 is no. 7100 with the 09.30 Birmingham to Poole. (J. Scrace)

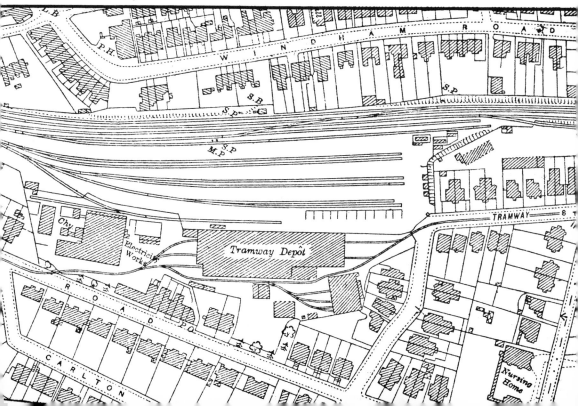

BOURNEMOUTH

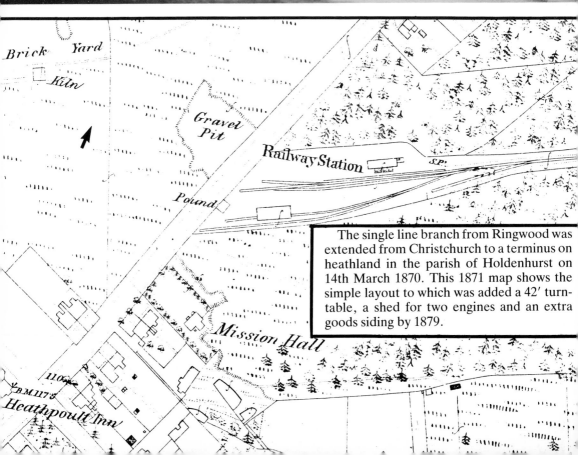

The single line branch from Ringwood was extended from Christchurch to a terminus on heathland in the parish of Holdenhurst on 14th March 1870. This 1871 map shows the simple layout to which was added a 42′ turntable, a shed for two engines and an extra goods siding by 1879.

111. A new station was opened on the opposite side of Holdenhurst Road on 20th July 1885, the original terminus being subsequently devoted entirely to goods traffic. At last there was a station worthy of this prosperous, expanding coastal resort.
(B.C. Vigor collection)

112. Known as Bournemouth East until 1st May 1899, the grander suffix "Central" was then bestowed on this mighty edifice. Passengers then crossed between platforms by a spacious but depressing subway. They now use an airy inelegant bridge. The railcar has already been described.
(B.C. Vigor collection)

113. An undated photograph taken from the road bridge bridge includes the short up bay, on the right, and Bournemouth Central 'A' Box on the left. This had been East Box in the LSWR era. (D. Cullum collection)

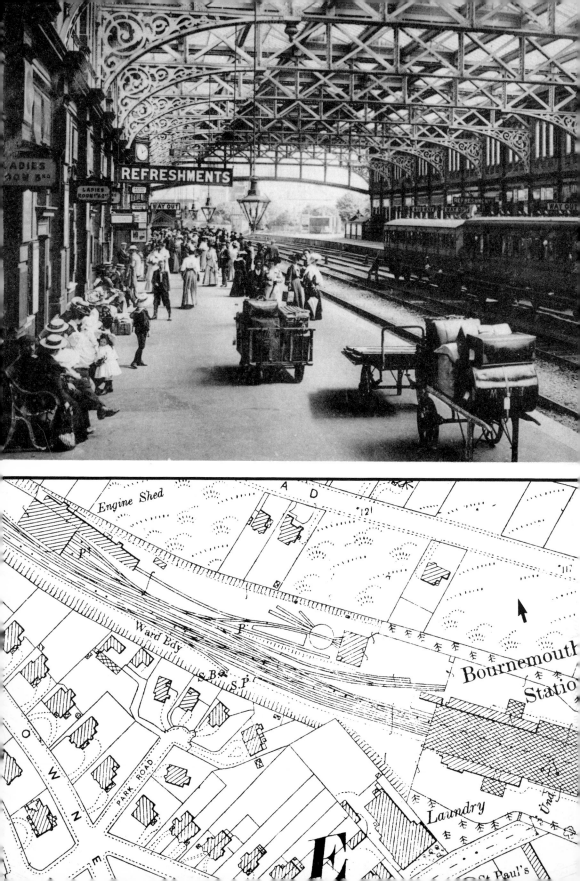

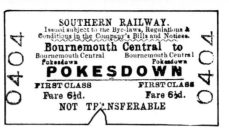

SOUTHERN RAILWAY.
Issued subject to the Bye-laws, Regulations & Conditions in the Company's Bills and Notices.

Bournemouth Central to

Bournemouth Central   Bournemouth Central
Pokesdown   Pokesdown

POKESDOWN

FIRST CLASS   FIRST CLASS
Fare 6½d.   Fare 6½d.

NOT TRANSFERABLE

0404   0404

London & South Western Ry.

TRICYCLE OR BATH CHAIR
When accompanied by passenger
BOURNEMOUTH EAST to
WATERLOO
Fare 5/-

S.1   See over

9559

114. Another eastward view shows more interesting social details, such as the need for class distinction in ladies toilets and the necessity of keeping one's head covered – preferably with a boater.
(D. Cullum collection)

   The 1898 edition shows the position of East and West Boxes, also the locomotive depot. The latter will be illustrated in a subsequent album, as it was to the east of the station.

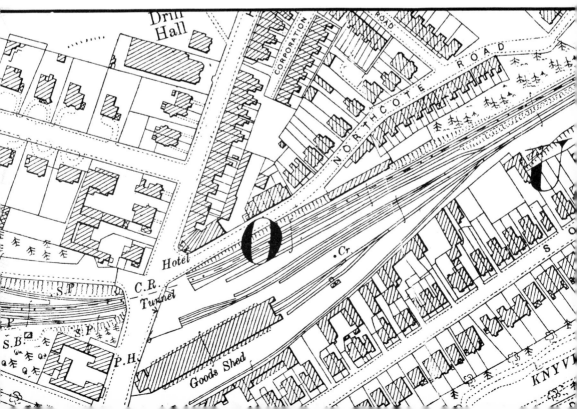

115. Class T9 no. 708, one of the "Greyhounds", makes a fine sight with the tidiness of inside bearings and motion. The detail of the wall finials and full end glazing to the train shed are worth noting, as they no longer exist. The photograph was taken on 11th September 1937. (J.G. Sturt)

117. On 12th July 1963, 2–6–0 no. 76008 was acting as station pilot and has just attached to the rear of a down arrival. The two centre roads would not be needed for electric services and so were removed in 1966. (C.L. Caddy)

116. The glazed area of the roof has been gradually reduced due to the high cost of repairs. Here we witness the departure of the up Bournemouth Belle on 22nd September 1962, in the capable hands of one of the rebuilt Bulleid Pacifics no. 35018 *British India Line*. After years in the scrap yard, this locomotive is undergoing restoration on the Mid-Hants Railway. (C.L. Caddy)

118. At the east end of the station trains pass under Holdenhurst Road by what most people regard as a bridge. Railway authorities have always described it as a 50 yard tunnel. A facing crossover behind no. 1840 enables up trains to depart from the down platform if necessary, both lines being signalled for reversible running through the station. (C. Hall)

SOUTHERN RAILWAY.
This ticket is not transferable and is issued subject to the Company's Bye-laws, Regulations and Conditions in their Time Tables, Notices and Book of Regulations.
Bournemouth West to
Bournemouth West   Bournemouth West
Bournemouth Ctl.   Bournemouth Ctl.
BOURNEMOUTH CTL.
First Class   First Class
Fare 8½d   Fare 8½d

119. The down platform was extended in 1928 to take two 12-coach trains. At the same time, the down bay and 'B' Box were dispensed with. This 60-lever signal box was then erected and now controls all movements from New Milton to Branksome Box. Class 33 no. 6513 waits for the arrival of an electric train from Waterloo so that it can take the leading coaches on to Weymouth. This operation ceases in 1988 when new air-conditioned "Silver Bullet" electric stock, with power-operated doors, will operate through to Weymouth. (C. Hall)

120. Having celebrated its centenary, the building is now under threat of demolition. Controversy rages as this historic, once elegant building, now life expired and inconvenient, awaits its fate. A 1978 picture shows no. 73001 on a Weymouth to Clapham Junction van train; 92, a semi-fast service for Waterloo and 93, a stopping train – two of three departures each hour forming the present excellent service to London. (J. Scrace)

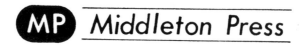

MP *Middleton Press*

Easebourne Lane, Midhurst, West Sussex, GU29 9AZ
☎ Midhurst (073 081) 3169

BRANCH LINES
BRANCH LINES TO MIDHURST   0 906520 01 0
BRANCH LINES TO HORSHAM   0 906520 02 9
BRANCH LINE TO SELSEY   0 906520 04 5
BRANCH LINES TO EAST GRINSTEAD   0 906520 07 X
BRANCH LINES TO ALTON   0 906520 11 8
BRANCH LINE TO HAYLING   0 906520 12 6
BRANCH LINE TO SOUTHWOLD   0 906520 15 0
BRANCH LINE TO TENTERDEN   0 906520 21 5
BRANCH LINES TO NEWPORT   0 906520 26 6
BRANCH LINES TO TUNBRIDGE WELLS   0 906520 32 0
BRANCH LINE TO SWANAGE   0 906520 33 9
BRANCH LINES AROUND GOSPORT   0 906520 36 3

SOUTH COAST RAILWAYS
BRIGHTON TO WORTHING   0 906520 03 7
WORTHING TO CHICHESTER   0 906520 06 1
CHICHESTER TO PORTSMOUTH   0 906520 14 2
BRIGHTON TO EASTBOURNE   0 906520 16 9
RYDE TO VENTNOR   0 906520 19 3
EASTBOURNE TO HASTINGS   0 906520 27 4
PORTSMOUTH TO SOUTHAMPTON   0 906520 31 2
HASTINGS TO ASHFORD   0 906520 37 1

SOUTHERN MAIN LINES
WOKING TO PORTSMOUTH   0 906520 25 8
HAYWARDS HEATH TO SEAFORD   0 906520 28 2
EPSOM TO HORSHAM   0 906520 30 4
CRAWLEY TO LITTLEHAMPTON   0 906520 34 7
THREE BRIDGES TO BRIGHTON   0 906520 35 5
WATERLOO TO WOKING   0 906520 38 X
VICTORIA TO EAST CROYDON   0 906520 40 1

STEAMING THROUGH
STEAMING THROUGH KENT   0 906520 13 4
STEAMING THROUGH EAST HANTS   0 906520 18 5
STEAMING THROUGH EAST SUSSEX   0 906520 22 3
STEAMING THROUGH SURREY   0 906520 39 8

OTHER RAILWAY BOOKS
WAR ON THE LINE
The official history of the SR in World War II   0 906520 10 X
GARRAWAY FATHER AND SON
The story of two careers in steam   0 906520 20 7

OTHER BOOKS
MIDHURST TOWN – THEN & NOW   0 906520 05 3
EAST GRINSTEAD – THEN & NOW   0 906520 17 7
THE MILITARY DEFENCE OF WEST SUSSEX   0 906520 23 1
WEST SUSSEX WATERWAYS   0 906520 24 X
BATTLE OVER PORTSMOUTH
A City at war in 1940   0 906520 29 0